MARKETING CRICUT FOR BEGINNERS

Learn How To Sell Your Creations In The Digital World

Craft Art Lab

Marketing Cricut for Beginners

© Copyright 2021 - All rights reserved.

The content contained within this book may not be reproduced, duplicated or transmitted without direct written permission from the author or the publisher.

Under no circumstances will any blame or legal responsibility be held against the publisher, or author, for any damages, reparation, or monetary loss due to the information contained within this book. Either directly or indirectly.

Legal Notice:

This book is copyright protected. This book is only for personal use. You cannot amend, distribute, sell, use, quote or paraphrase any part, or the content within this book, without the consent of the author or publisher.

Disclaimer Notice:

Marketing Cricut for Beginners

Please note the information contained within this document is for educational and entertainment purposes only. All effort has been executed to present accurate, up to date, and reliable, complete information. No warranties of any kind are declared or implied. Readers acknowledge that the author is not engaging in the rendering of legal, financial, medical or professional advice. The content within this book has been derived from various sources. Please consult a licensed professional before attempting any techniques outlined in this book.

By reading this document, the reader agrees that under no circumstances is the author responsible for any losses, direct or indirect, which are incurred as a result of the use of information contained within this document, including, but not limited to, — errors, omissions, or inaccuracies.

Table Of Contents

Introduction	6
Is Cricut so Amazing as They say?	10
Tools that you need to start immediately	13
Cutting and blades– all you need to know about	17
Tricks to clean your Mats	18
Cutting Blades	19
German Carbide Blade	20
Deep Cut Blade	21
Pens	21
The Cricut Engraving Tip	22
The Fine Debossing Tip	22
The Basic Perforation Blade	23
The Wavy Blade	24
Cricut Design Space: Explained- Terminology- Account Creation- Mobile device	25

Marketing Cricut for Beginners

Cricut Design Space	25
Cricut Design Space Terminology for Beginners	28
Design Space on mobile devices	39
Design Space Canvas	41
Cartridge Overview	44
Cricut Design Studio	48
How to approach with Vinyl	51
Using Snap Mat cutting multiple Colors	52
How to create an offset image on Inkscape	60
How to do layering using self adhesive vinyl	63
How to deal with Wood	65
The Design Space is an Internet application that helps companies develop business strategies.	70
Cricut for Business	84
Cricut Business has exploded through the digital world!	87
Brainstorming Section	91

Marketing your Cricut	**95**
Understanding E-Commerce in Your Cricut Business	**98**
It is possible to create your own design on the Design Space with ease.	**103**
When choosing what crafts to sell, there are a few points to consider	**107**
Selecting supplies for business	**113**
How to Choose the perfect Name for your Cricut Business	**114**
E- commerce Store – Build your own	**124**
Refund Policy	**128**
How to make your business bigger.	**132**

Introduction

Find your inner maker with handmade goods. There is nothing more satisfying than buying an original item, different from any other products on the market and crafted by someone who really cares about their product.

People are starting to see that manufactured items might not be as good-quality or true to themselves as they think because craftsmanship in so many areas has gone down over time due to low wages and poor working conditions for craftsmen around the world. In the last years, there was a radical shift in the orientation of several buyers, buyers prefer to make a different choice, they want to make a smart decision... instead of purchasing items manufactured on big scales, they choose to purchase crafted, vintage items.

Cricut is actually a machine that permits to transform your dreams to reality. You are able to cut a large number of supplies such as papers, vinyl, cards of any type and textures. You can create invitations for your friends make a nice t-shirt...

Marketing Cricut for Beginners

Not only are people becoming more environmentally conscious and choosing to purchase made-to-order items, but they also want to make a "smart" decision. The Cricut is one machine that is making this possible by cutting out the middleman with regards to production and allowing individuals who have never before had access or knowledge of design software, cut their own materials at home in order create everything from invitations for friends' birthdays parties all the way up through professional designer clothing pieces.

Cricut is actually a machine that permits to transform your dreams to reality. You are able to cut a large number of supplies such as papers, vinyl, cards of any type and textures. You can create invitations for your friends make a nice t-shirt...

It really works with an internet application called the Design Space. There is no limit to what you can do with this machine, and with the help of this software you are able to create, upload and also buy a design that you can shape and size and resize as much as you like.

Marketing Cricut for Beginners

Imagine if you could create your own custom design for any occasion, without the need to know how to draw. With a Cricut machine and special Design Space software- there are no limits! You can make anything from shirts or pillows with unique designs that will be personalized just for you.

The Design Space will allow you to browse tons of different designs and then customize them in a variety of ways. You can make the font bigger or smaller, change the color scheme, even add words! There are so many options that it is really hard to choose which one makes your creative juices flow more (although there isn't an easy way).

When you upload your design on Design Space, they ask for the information about what kind of material you want to use: t-shirt printable fabric? cotton canvas? something else like wall art? They also let us know if we need anything extra such as interfacing or stabilizers but don't worry because those items will be available from your side .

Marketing Cricut for Beginners

It's really easy to use, you just have to click on the color palette and choose one of the colors that suit your design. You can also upload an image which will be easier for those who are more visual, but if you want something original then it is better to create something from scratch!

Design Space offers a lot so take some time in exploring all its features and don't forget that this machine does not limit what we can do with our imagination and creativity!

 As long as we stay patient, Design Space always helps us find our way out of any creative block .

Is Cricut so Amazing as They say?

There are so many creative things you can do with a Cricut Machine. For all of the newbies, here is an overview on some famous tasks that one can complete using this amazing machine!

The first one is cutting and scoring any material. It can be a paper, cardstock, vinyl or even fabric!

Next up is the use of stencils like lace patterns for example. A Cricut Machine has the ability to cut through all sorts of materials with precision without leaving an uneven edge on your design. And last but not least- The Cricut machine also offers other purposes such as gluing surfaces together by using heat activated glue in order to create decorations from different kinds of materials that will stick permanently!

Marketing Cricut for Beginners

Each task can be designed out and saved within Design Space which works as a virtual art studio that lets you shape and size it how ever you want while having options for various colors too!

Here are some projects that will help you finally put your Cricut skills to good use. From designing and creating Christmas decorations, ornaments, t-shirts (or other fabric), addressing an envelope for a handmade card - there's something here for everyone! Cut out letters or shapes with precision using the craft knife on scrapbooking paper. Design vinyl stickers, stencils of paintings while also adding design inscription onto plates cups and mugs as well as engraving designs into glassware such create personalized gifts like memory glasses etched with a loved one's name in script font matching their handwriting style so they can always have them close by when drinking coffee each morning before beginning work at 9am sharp every single day without fail.

Marketing Cricut for Beginners

Design Space has truly changed the way that people design and create their own creations. No longer do you need to pay a high price for something original, made with love by hand - instead it is right at your fingertips! Design space makes it possible to be artistic even without any prior experience or skills in art and drawing. It doesn't matter what age group you are from (children, adults) there's something here for everyone! Let the creativity flow through these amazing tools on this app-based machine! This will make designing items so much easier than before when all they had was paper and pencils-- now anything is possible: painting designs onto fabric (), addressing an envelope for a handmade card - there's something here for everyone!

Tools that you need to start immediately

Each one of us has different ways to bring our ideas to life. You might want more resources for making projects. These are some of the things you could use:

-Paper, pen and pencils

-Computer with design software

-Crayons, markers, paints

-Scissors

You need new tools if you are using a Cricut. You will love your tool set.

I love Cricut. You can get a toolset that has all the resources together for less money. It is good if you have different prices in your pocket. Having a variety of change is very important. If you are out of change, people may not want to do business with you because they don't like dealing with small bills and coins.

Marketing Cricut for Beginners

The Cricut Essential Tool Set comes with 7 different tools. It's great for scrapbookers, card makers, and crafters, plus a scoring blade and extra replacement blade for your portable trimmer.

It's available in mint (pictured), blue or rose. It retails for $49.99 but if you are not in rush to have it, you will see that it goes on sale often.

1. Cricut Scraper Tool – this tool with the Cricut Spatula Tool will scrape out paper, card and even vinyl. The scraper tool helps remove unwanted scraps from your cutting mat which is helpful for intricate cuttings that can easily get messy. You'll be very grateful when you want to place your new vinyl on a project but it's all scratched up so much!

2. Cricut Tweezers are the perfect tool for picking up those tiny little pieces and getting them secured in place.

Marketing Cricut for Beginners

3. The Cricut Scissors are the perfect item for cutting. The blades have a micro tip that is easy to use and can cut through materials with ease, unlike other scissors which require more force in order to get them working properly. Additionally, these scissors feature an included blade cover so you don't accidentally cut your fingers or any sensitive areas while using them!

4. The Cricut Spatula is a sturdy tool with an angled head that makes it perfect for lifting cut images off the mat. It's uniquely shaped design can help to avoid tearing fragile material and will come in handy when you have difficult cuts - especially if they are ones where stability matters!

5. Cricut Scoring Stylus– The stylus is used to produce neat fold lines for boxes, cards, envelopes, and also your 3D projects. It's placed in the A slot of your machine. You can make beautiful card envelopes with the Cricut Scoring Stylus. It is placed in slot A, and it gives you perfect folds every time!

6. The Cricut Weeder is the perfect tool to have on hand when you are working with small pieces of vinyl and other iron-on projects. It makes removing any tiny cuts or unwanted bits a breeze, saving so much time for your project!

7. Portable Trimmer- This is the one tool you can't miss for getting accurate straight lines and a perfect edge on your mat. I adore cutting my vinyl so that it matches up perfectly with this little guy. You will also get 2 replacement blades in the pack to keep those clean cuts coming!

2: Create an original work of art, such as writing or drawing from scratch, inspired by what we just read together (don't worry about quality).

Cutting and blades– all you need to know about

Cutting Mats

Cutting mats are essential for paper-cutting projects. 3 types of cutting mats exist: the light grip, standard grip and strong grips mat. The light grip is best when you use it with lightweight materials like letter paper or vellum; whereas a standard gripping mat can be used on thinner items such as typical cardstock or vinyl while ensuring that the knife does not slip off easily from your hands onto delicate surfaces below which could cause damage to them in case they were cut by accident. For thicker material like glitter card stock, heavy fabric and chipboard there is always strong gripper designed for more sturdy pieces that need precision cuts without any possible accidents happening during usage. You can't miss it!

Tricks to clean your Mats

Cleaning your mat regularly is essential to retain its stickiness. This means that you should give it a light cleaning when the surface begins to lose some of this quality. Cleaning with soap and water, wiping off any dirt using baby wipes or spraying degreaser on an extremely dirty one will keep it sticky for as long as possible!

Using baby wipes will help you gently clean the mat without harming it. This can be done by wetting down the surface, removing debris and then wiping with soap and water for a normal cleaning or using a degreaser if your mats are extremely dirty.

Fortunately, there is a solution for this problem. You can clean and dry your mat in order to replenish the stickiness of it. When you buy the Cricut Machine, which includes cutting mats inside of its box if necessary (unless you have another need), then all will be well!

-The mat gets dirty and loses the stickiness on its surface.

-This problem can be solved with a couple of tricks that are not complicated at all:

o Cleaning it with a degreaser or by using baby wipes will take care of most dirt, as well as wetting down the surface in order to remove debris from your cutting area before wiping off any soap residue. You can also use water only for an easy cleaning if you don't need anything stronger than plain old H20!

o If the mat is really dirty and sticky, then you should wait until it dries thoroughly before returning to your workstation. This includes letting it air dry outside overnight.

Cutting Blades

The Cricut Machine is a device that includes nearly all the tools necessary to make your own cards, labels and other crafts. One of those essential blades are included in this tool but it can become blunt after some time so you will want extra on hand for when need arises. Two more types are available on market. The one you will get is strong and sharp, but it is always good to have extra blades on hand because after a while the blade becomes blunt.

German Carbide Blade

The blade has a sharp edge that can cut through tough materials. It lasts a long time because of its durability and is made out of stainless steel, which holds up against rust.

Deep Cut Blade

You can cut more than 50 materials with this one tool! It's also used to sharpen the blades. Learning how to use it could make your old blade last even longer and decrease the need for buying new ones as often.

Pens

Using your Cricut Machine is like writing in a blank notebook. You can make use of the many free fonts, and purchase from their library if you wish to as well. And for those who have other fonts on their computer that they want to use, this isn't an issue either!

The Cricut Engraving Tip

The Cricut Engraving Tip will allow you to produce personalized monograms and texts. In addition, it can create ornamental embellishments such as flourishes or quotes of your choice that are engraved on a keepsake. You're able to make customized title plates with this tool, in the style of wood sculptures or jewelry. It is recommended for use with "aluminum flat metal," but other materials work well too (natural leathers and acrylic) when used alongside them!

The Fine Debossing Tip

The Cricut Maker has a number of techniques to help you create some amazing paper crafts. You can use it for sharp debossed designs, dimensional cards, monogrammed thank-you paperwork and more! It's the perfect tool if you're looking for that pro finish or even additional elevation on your starting material. With "coated papers", shimmery silver cardstock or glitter newspaper - this tip will be just what gives them an incredible impact with minimal work from all! You are able to purchase the "Fine Debossing Tip" for 24.99 dollars.

The Basic Perforation Blade

This blade makes it easy to make intricate perforated designs and uniform lines that are perfect for raffle tickets, journals, holiday decorations or more. It is also great with things like cardstock, foam paper and foil! You can use this knife just by using your "Cricut Maker" machine. You can get the "Basic Perforation Blade " for 29.99 dollars.

The Wavy Blade

This blade can be used with iron-on, vinyl, paper, and fabric. It can also be used on cardstock. You should use it with the "Cricut Maker" machine.

This blade is made out of stainless steel and it has a wavy edge. It can be used to make original vinyls, iron on stickers, envelopes, cards, present tags, and collage projects.

This beautifully crafted stainless steel blade is actually perfect for "creating original vinyl decals, iron on styles, envelopes, cards and collage projects". Or perhaps when you're trying to add a fashionable edge with an artistic wavy finish to the crafting of yours. It will help you cut decorative edges much quicker than drag cutting tool while providing efficiently molded cuts across wide range of tasks.

Cricut Design Space: Explained- Terminology- Account Creation- Mobile device

Cricut Design Space

Marketing Cricut for Beginners

The Cricut Design Space app is a fantastic software that will make you feel like an artist. With it, you can create and cut your own projects for the Explore or other cutting machines from scratch or with pre-made templates. You'll be able to access all of your information anywhere without having to worry about carrying around any discs!

You can start a task on your phone whenever the motivation strikes and choose it right up from your laptop because the software program is synchronized across all of your devices.

Save your space and money by linking a physical cartridge to Cricut Design Space. This way, the digital versions of those images are activated on your account with no extra cost from buying cartridges in stores or even online!

Imagine you are working on your project, but suddenly feel like the Internet connection is out. With the Cricut Design Space software and a device that can store fonts or pictures, save yourself from having to do all of these things over again! You'll be able to make decorations for any occasion; stylish accessories; scrapbooks - even wedding invitations with just one easy-to-use program.

Marketing Cricut for Beginners

When you're crafting away and life gets in the way of your internet connection, don't worry! The Cricut Design Space software enables you to continue developing so that no matter how much time passes by without an internet connection while making projects such as party or holiday crafts for friends and family.

Cut all the crafts of yours with a Cricut Explore or Maker device. You have more than 50 thousand pictures, projects and fonts to choose from on the Image Library. With your own personalized designs published for free you are able to cut thicker materials like fabric, poster board and cardstock-iron-on as well as vinyl paper.

Remember, Cricut Design Space is compatible with Cricut Maker, Cricut Explore, Cricut Explore Air, Cricut Explore One, and Cricut Explore Air 2. I recommend you to use a high-speed broadband internet connection. It will work very well with Firefox®, Microsoft Edge

Apple Safari®, Google Chrome®, Mozilla®, but you won'see it working with Internet Explorer.

If you're a complete beginner with the Cricut Machine, then this table will be perfect for you. But if your proficiency level is higher than that of an amateur and have been using it extensively before, then take this guide along to ensure any doubts are cleared up or use as occasional reminders on what to do next in certain situations.

Cricut Design Space Terminology for Beginners

The Cricut machine and Design Space software can be a little daunting at first. After all, the only thing you want to do is jump into tutorials but before doing that it's important to get familiar with some of the terminology so you know what everything means when there are instructions telling how to use them.

This post will introduce you to some of the terms in Design Space. It is a useful resource for beginners who are just getting started using their Cricut machine and navigating this environment! the top of the screen in Design Space, you will see a banner with several buttons on it. These are your Navigation Tools and they provide access to important features within this software that may be used for any number of purposes.

Marketing Cricut for Beginners

Learn how various tools work by first clicking and holding down on them to highlight their names before releasing so that you know what each button does!

Cricut Parts Library: Now let's start with some terminology related to Cricut parts. In order to make something from scratch (or upload an image) into a cutting machine-ready file, we must first have images or texts saved as files onto our computer hard drive which can then be uploaded via USB cable connection or shared online through Google Drive.

Attach

 It lets you lets you attach notes to images, hold images, and write on top of image.

Align

This function aligns the items of a list based on the user's selection.

Arrange

The image can be moved to any position by dragging its corners.

Marketing Cricut for Beginners

Color Sync

Color Sync panel helps match colors from one project to another. This way you don't have to use many different materials or colors of materials when you are cutting the material.

Canvas

The canvas is where you design. It's not blank, but it has lots of tools. You can use these to design and make things!

Contour

The Contour tool lets you hide portions of an image layer quickly so that they won't cut out.

Cut lines

When you have a shape, or layer that has multiple outlines and want to cut them each out separately, then the way is that firstly drag your mouse across all the lines of shapes. Then make sure you click "Cut".

Cut Button

Marketing Cricut for Beginners

The Cricut cut button is one of the core buttons for your machine, which will initiate a cutting.

The Cut Screen a.k.a Make it Button

The screen that appears after clicking the "make it" button. You can watch your design come to life as you use a custom cutter on fabric, paper or vinyl!

Cutting Mat

A cutting mat is a flat surface that you put your material on top of to load it into the Cricut machine.

Deselect All

Clear all of the things that are already picked on your canvas.

Design Space

Cricut's software is good for making and designing things. You can do it all on the cloud.

Delete

Delete will remove an image from the canvas.

Marketing Cricut for Beginners

Draw Lines

Draw lines or writing will be the line type when using a pen to write script or draw an image.

Duplicate

If you want to copy something that you see on the screen, then just press "Ctrl" and "C".

Edit Bar

The edit button allows you to cut and paste any object on the canvas.

Flip

Turn an image 180 degrees horizontally or vertically.

Fill

An image is a pattern or print that goes on the canvas.

Flatten

Marketing Cricut for Beginners

Flattening means that a current vector, which has 2 or more layers can be turned into a printable image. It is like a picture for you.

Group

Group command enables multiple image layers or text present on the canvas to be selected and move at one time as one object so not to affect their layout.

Images or Image Library

Images that you can buy or use for free in the Cricut membership or freebie section of Design Space.

JPG & PNG Files

These are image files that will end in either .jpeg or .png. These are uploaded in Design Space for the Print and Cut feature.

Linetype

The linetype is the action that will occur when the Cricut machine creates – cut, draw and score are the 3 options.

Marketing Cricut for Beginners

Load Button

The load button is the double arrow button present next to the cut button on the machine. This will be pressed to load and unload the cutting mat from the machine.

Layers (Panel)

Layers refer to one unified image on the canvas. Multiple images can be "layered" together or moved backward and forward.

Material Settings

Material settings are present in Design Space or on the dial or the Explore machine. These are key to setting the pressure that the blade will use on the selected material.

Mirrored Image

Marketing Cricut for Beginners

Mirroring your design can be tricky on the computer, but it's a breeze to do in-person with heat transfer vinyl. To mirror an image you need to reverse its colors so that when they are transferred onto the garment or other material, everything will appear right way up and readable. The easy function for this is found on our cut screens - just select "mirror" from their dropdown menu!

No Fill

No fill means that there is no print pattern present on the vector selected on the canvas.

Print then cut

A flattened image on the canvas often with a pattern (or color fill) will be sent to your home printer via Design Space and then an outline of that printed image cut by the machine.

Registration Marks

Guides that are printed when using the print and cut function. Cricut reads these as a means of cutting the flattened image correctly.

Redo

Marketing Cricut for Beginners

Redo a recent action that was undone when working in Design Space.

Reverse Weeding

Reverse weeding removed the vinyl that would normal be left behind. This is used generally for stencil vinyl.

Rotate

Rotate any image 360 degrees on the canvas.

Select All

The select all button allows you to actively select any images presently visible on the canvas.

Score Lines

Score lines are creasing the paper or material used with a scoring tool or wheel. They can be found under the shapes button.

Size

The size is the dimensions of an image or object when selected on the canvas.

Marketing Cricut for Beginners

Slice

The slice tool created new cut paths from 2 images. It will result in 3 or more new shapes that present as new layers.

Shapes

Shapes button allows you to insert any basic geometric shape onto your canvas

SVG (a.k.a Scalable Vector Graphic)

An SVG cut file is a vector graphic that can be scaled larger or smaller and still retain resolution. It's made up of infinitely small lines; when put together they create intricate designs, like one you might see in the background of open source software projects!

Text or Font

Text is how you can type words and customize your writing with special fonts and scripts within Design Space.

Ungroup

Ungrouping enables you to move each layer of a vector on the canvas individual from its counterparts.

Undo

Undo a recent action in Design Space.

Upload

Upload is when you add your own vector, print or pattern fill images to Design Space.

Weld

The weld tool enables you to combine 2 single shapes into one new shape for a single cut line. Welding is often used with text to create seamless cursive words.

Weeding

The process of removing unwanted excess vinyl from a cut design.

How to create an account on www.cricut.com

1. From the top right corner of the screen of the official site of Cricut, select "Design".

2. From the bottom of the screen a new window will come out, select "Create a Cricut Id".

3. Enter your personal information.

4. Accept the Cricut Terms of Use and "Create a Cricut ID".

5. You will drop to the "Design Space" landing page and you will see the message displayed "New! Set your machine mode".

With these 5 steps your registration is completed.

The next step is to hit the green Next button and select whichever machine you have. If it's a Cricut Maker, then choose "Maker" from the right side of your screen; for all others, just pick what type of cutting mat or materials are yours (e.g., Vinyl Sheets). Then go ahead and create!

Design Space on mobile devices

The Cricut Design Space is available for Android and you can download it from Google Store

Marketing Cricut for Beginners

And in the Apple Store for your iOS device. When running the Cricut Design Space for the first time you will be guided from the App Overview to help you to set up the app. It will be helpful also if you need help in the usage of the app with your mobile phone.

Cricut's new app allows you to create, edit and share projects from your phone. The image library offers over two million images that can be used for any project imaginable; the panel control gives users a wealth of options in editing their work as well as previewing or printing it on mat board with crisply cut edges. With instant access to all Cricut cartridges digitally available through purchase at an affordable price, this is one device that will never go out-of-date!

- Design Space is an application that will help you to create anything - shapes, decorations, logos and more. You can use it for your personal projects or commercially too.

There are many apps available on the App Store and Google Play stores with similar features as this one, but the difference between them all is in their design: Design space is a bit different from other applications because of its interface which has been tailored not only to suit users who have little experience using computers but also those who need simplicity when creating designs. The app includes tutorials so even beginners can easily understand how everything works!

This software enables people of any level operate without difficulty through its intuitive tools.

Design Space Canvas

The Canvas is an open source document processor that makes designing documents a breeze. It's not only for writers, but also for artists as well!

Getting started with your Canvas

Design Panel

On the left side of your Panel you will find the tool bar with the following options:

Marketing Cricut for Beginners

New – By clicking on this icon, a new project window will open.

Templates – In the first step, you are able to visualize your final project in real-life background.

Projects – The "Projects" tab is an important part of Shopify because it's where you can find, select and manage all your projects.

Images – You are able to find several different images for free in the Cricut Image Library, including your own ones.

Text – Click the Text to add your favorite words and phrases that you want to use into Canvas.

Shapes – By clicking this tab you are able to add basic shapes like squares, circles, triangles, and also score lines into your Canvas.

Upload – You are able to cut and modify all the images you wish and you can upload format like: .jpg, .gif, .png, .bmp, .svg, or .dxf image files without getting charged.

Header

Marketing Cricut for Beginners

On the top of the screen at your left you are able to find the **Menu** to access to the features such as Home, Link Cartridges, Settings, Help, Etc. You are able to find the Sign Out option, too.

Page Title – To help you to keep in mind which page in Design Space you are on. If you click on the Page Title you are able to close an open tab.

Project Name- Here to see the name of your project and if you have unsaved projects, it will say Untitled.

My Projects – Open one of your projects that you previously saved.

Save – It's easy to keep your project on the go by saving it in your account. You can access this saved project across any device and you will be able to see a list of projects when accessing from different devices or even sites!

Make It – When you are ready to transfer your project to your Cricut Machine after you have prepared your mats, you can click Make it.

Zoom

Zoom in to see your projects more clearly. Or, Zoom out to have a general view of all the tasks you need to do.

Cartridge Overview

What are your favorites Cricut Cartridges to buy? Here is a list of the most popular ones!

What's your favorite type of cartridge for you and why not share it with us in our comments section below.

Disney Mickey Font Cricut Cartridge

Cricut Disney Frozen Cartridge

Cricut Cartridge Disney Dreams Come True

Cricut Cartridge Classically Modern Cards

Cricut Home Decor Vinyl Wall Cartridge

Cricut Decorate

Cricut Cartridge Simple Pop Up Cards

Cricut Cartridge French Manor

Marketing Cricut for Beginners

It's always a good idea to share your cartridges, but there are other ways of doing this too. If you own an older model Cricut machine like the Gypsy and have multiple copies of one cartridge - it can be useful in some situations for others not lucky enough to own their very first copy! You might even want to take your gypsy with you when attending crafting events as they're often left at home on account that people travel light nowadays.

Cricut recently announced that they are retiring all physical cartridges. This means that you will only be able to use your Cricut machines for new digital or old cartridge designs through the Design Space software (Cricur Explore and Maker)*.

*Older Cricuts can still communicate with a computer but not any more with other cartridges.

The Cricut machine is the perfect tool for getting creative and imaginative with your crafting projects. One of a kind cartridges enable you to get as creative or crazy as you want!

The general classes of Cricut Cartridges are:

Marketing Cricut for Beginners

Font cartridge: The left side of the page is a bright green, with images and drawings on it. The right side has text in different fonts, all delicately arranged into shapes to form words that say "Happy Birthday," or "I love you."

The cartridge I'm looking for isn't anything like what's there! It contains total letters, numbers and pictures alongside style type texts- some seasonal cartridges include Forever Young (green), Lyrical Letters (pink), Jasmine(blue) Pumpkin Carving for Halloween (orange); Teardrop: Thanksgiving Holiday; Winter Wonderland for Christmas season, etc

Shape cartridge: This one has many shapes, such as boxes, tags, animals and sports. It also has paper dolls.

Licensed cartridge: Cutting hair with cartoon characters is no longer just for kids. Adult clients can now visit the most popular cutting salon in Tokyo and enjoy a haircut from their favorite character, such as Hello Kitty or Mickey Mouse.

Marketing Cricut for Beginners

Classmate cartridge: as the name proposes, is explicitly designed for study hall purposes, which highlights classroom fonts, classroom design, shapes, visual study plan, ideas and sayings teachers, etc.

Solutions cartridge: The Cricut has a variety of cutting options that can be used to create an endless amount of crafts. The designs include Welding, Soccer, Baseball and more. With the help from their wide range of cartridges crafters are able not only explore different craft materials but also experiment with shapes including round or square cutouts for cards!

For the person who is passionate about paper crafts and scrapbooks, a nice way to add even more creativity into your work would be with cutout designs and shapes. Luckily there are cartridges available for that too! But if you enjoy focusing mainly on words as well, then text style might be just the thing for you.

Cricut Design Studio

Cricut's software suite is full of amazing features, from thousand different design options to surprising capacities and structures. It offers you the ability to plan for your kids' craft ideas, family get-togethers, or friends special occasions with ease.

With the Cricut Design Studio Software, any person that doesn't have technical experience of a CAD program can cut out shapes and letters with ease! The software even comes equipped with clip art like animals or flowers for those who want to make their own cutesy scrapbook pages.

The company has made it easier than ever before to create your own scrapbooks by introducing the Cricut Expression Home Cutting Machine! With this machine you don't need an artistic background because all you do is input what shape, lettering style, font etc., then hit one button on your screen and voila - instant masterpiece (or at least close enough)!

Marketing Cricut for Beginners

The Cricut software takes the already inventive machine to an even more creative level. The design database is accessible from your home computer, which means you can create any shape or letter in the cartridge library quickly and easily without a tedious search through different shapes.

The Cricut Design Studio Software is a perfect tool for those who want to create their own designs and images. It offers the ever-growing library of fonts, shapes, stencils and more that range from simple letters to full phrases - enabling you complete control over your machine before it even starts cutting! With an updated online database that is constantly being added on too with new font choices every day, there's no better time than now get started designing!

If you're in need of a fresh and new idea, the Cricut Design Studio has got your back. Check out items from their message sheets or search for creative documents created by other clients on the web to spice up your own designs with some new style!

Marketing Cricut for Beginners

It's easy to create complex structures when you use more than one cartridge. You'll need to have all materials accessible, but the end result will be worth it! Make various layers for your design, like shadows and different elements of a picture. The key is that every layer needs its own cut in the software so that each component can be created independently on preferred paper by Cricut machine.

The Cricut Design Studio Software is $60 and it's a good idea for people who like Cricuts. The software will help you make a lot of things that you can't do without the software.

How to approach with Vinyl

There are different types of vinyl that you can use.

There are different types of vinyl that you can use.

Oracal 651, is a type of the more permanent adhesive and if used in any other way might compromise your surface or leave residue behind which would not be ideal for an indoor creation like mugs, plates, bowls. But this may vary depending on what one person needs so it's best to go with a smaller project first before using these materials elsewhere knowing they will make heavy work out of them such as outdoor displays where water resistance is necessary!

Oracal 631 is a type of vinyl that can be used for wall decals, stencils and other artsy projects. It's not as durable when applied to something like the outside of your car or on furniture because it scratches easily but you can use this product in infinite ways: phone cases, interior decorations...

Heat Transfer Vinyl (More known as HTV)

You can customize your favorite clothing with this easy to apply and durable technique. The most popular iron on vinyl is Scissor EasyWeed, which you cut out after following the instructions in this guide.

Easy to use, it comes in a variety of styles and colors and it holds up through the washing machine, it looks perfect. It is ideal for: Socks, T-shirts, Stuffed animals, Canvas tote bags, Costumes, anything with fabric

Printable Vinyl

Printable Vinyl comes both in Heat Transfer and Adhesive types. All you need to have with this particular material is a normal inkjet printer, and the design can be printed out on your vinyl.

Using Snap Mat cutting multiple Colors

Marketing Cricut for Beginners

What would you like to create? Decorate your mat with the different colors of vinyl- or maybe even use it for a table runner. Whatever project you choose, take pieces of vinyl and cut them all up into squares that are about 3x3 inches big. Lay out these little squares on your Cricut Mat (or any surface) so they're easy to see when taking pictures! Next, from within the Cricut App click Projects in the Cloud>Projects List>Customize Project>, then replace whatever is already there with what ever text/image file(s)/shape(es) want to cut out onto fabric using my machine's blade>. Finally, hit Make It- this will prepare everything needed before to start.

Once the picture popped up, select use, and then select continue. You can start your creation with multiple colors in one mat. You can create images and text and swipe from one color to another.

You can change the color of your vinyl with a single click. Once you have positioned all of them, go to Cricut and cut it out!

Marketing Cricut for Beginners

When we begin designing our image or text onto one layer over different colors, clicking on the three dots will allow us to select which map that we want our chosen piece in. If for instance I wanted my design hovering above green but not below red then this would be helpful - by selecting move to another map under blue (which displays as unused) before switching back up top into position again over pink-red where desired; now both layers are visible from their individual maps so there is no need for scrolling anymore between each other when positioning images/text like previously mentioned because they're right nextrome OS: As an operating system, Chrome is pretty interesting. You can use it on any computer as long as there's a browser and you have internet access. It has a few advantages over your average Windows or MacOS settings but also some disadvantages that would be worth considering before switching to the popular Google-made system for all of your needs - one advantage being the way in which they handle data security and encryption because of how heavily involvement with web content they're involved-

Marketing Cricut for Beginners

Everyone loves buying something original, anything completely different as opposed to the others, to own something true and made with passion and love. Crafted items are starting to be very popular each day, and therefore they are more and more replacing wide manufactured products.

Changing the blade on your Cricut

It's time to change out the blade on your Cricut. First, make sure that you have unplugged and turned off the machine! Once it is safe for us to carry-on with our work inside of this miraculous device, flip open Accessory Clamp B (which will be used exclusively for blades). Notice how there are two clamps: one labeled "A" which we'll use later when switching pens or other accessories; and another labelled "B," as in Blade. After flipping down accessory clamp B's silver plunger allllllmost at once while also keeping a firm grip around its housing - you may notice an unexpected feeling –this stuff IS pretty cool afterall—you can then remove blade.

Gently pull the blade straight out, and hold the silver plunger at the same time.

Marketing Cricut for Beginners

To load a new blade, simply remove the rubber covering and push the new blade into the slot. There is a magnet inside the blade house, so it should pull the blade right in.

Return the silver blade housing to the cut smart carriage inside the Cricut machine and close the accessory clamp.

Done it!

Let's see few features of Cricut machine that you will love.

The Cricut Design Space is a great way to make your projects the way you want. You can upload your own images and it is free!

You can upload your own images to use in Cricut Design Space. This is FREE, and allows you creative flexibility with what the design will look like on paper or fabric! Simply click the Upload tab and follow prompts for a smooth process that's easy as pie.

The Cricut writes beautifully with pens- I was able to create so many projects because of this tool alone! In fact, gone are the days of handwriting countless envelopes; my life has been made much easier by using beautiful font via pen from within my computer screen thanks to these wonderful tools.

Cricut Access is a monthly subscription. This subscription provides you with access to hundreds of fonts and thousands of images. Cricut Access has three tiers:

Cricut Access Fonts – provides access to hundreds of fonts.

Cricut access standard means that you can use different fonts and images. It also offers 10% off on digital and physical products.

Cricut Access Premium provides you with access to hundreds of fonts, thousands of images, and a 10% discount on physical purchases and a 50% discount on digital purchases.

How to regulate depth of the blade

To adjust the pressure of the blade:

Open Design Space. Go to the left top of your screen, and click on your name. Then go into Manage Custom Materials. The top you will see Dial Presets - you can increase or decrease here easily.

How to regulate the speed of your cutting in Cricut

With the Cricut, you cannot change the speed but you can change the pressure. You need to set it on vinyl and then start cutting.

How to create an SVG File

A lot of people get confused and have no clue on how to create a SVG file, so I thought it might be really useful for you to find it in this guide.

First of all, you need to find your free vectors in:

###a href="https://www.clipartmax.com/" rel="noopener noreferrer" target="_blank">https://www.clipartmax.com/

Or here,

https://pixabay.com/

Or here,

https://unsplash.com/

Then you can go into the website
https://svgcreator.com/

Then convert your file into SVG and download your new file!

How to create an offset image on Inkscape

Download your favorite image in png.

Having a png image means having a transparent background, so that means that when you open your image you will be able to see only the image without squares or white or black backgrounds, but only the image itself.

Once you downloaded your image you can open your Cricut Design Space and click upload images from the left bar.

There is a nice program that I want to show you, that is Inkscape, and it is free.

Once you open the program and drag the image into the Inkscape Pad. Immediately will come up this advice below, you can just leave it and press Ok.

Marketing Cricut for Beginners

Click create text, select the whole text, go back to the path and click Union. When you click this button will mean that you just weld the text.

Click on the path again, scroll down to linked offset now, a small white square will appear on one of the letters, we call it node.

Pick a color for the shadow or offset. If you put the cursor on that square and drag it a little it will create the offset or the shadow the size that you want.

On the left side panel, click on the cursor tool then move the text below. Click the path nodes tool and you will see the nodes on the text now.

Click on the shadow and then go back up to the path and click object to path. The shadow will show you the path nodes. Select the cursor tool again and move the text back to the shadow, select both and select object, scroll down and click on align and distribute.

On the right side of the screen will pop up a window that let you choose how to align the text. You select both and click on object, then group.

Marketing Cricut for Beginners

Now go to file, save as, name the file and save it as a plain SVG. Then go to Cricut Design space to upload your file, name the file and click save. Click on the image and click insert. Then you go ahead and ungroup the image and there you go. That's how you create an offset text on Inkscape.

How to do layering using self adhesive vinyl

Let see now how to do layering by using self-adhesive vinyl. You will need 4 layers with a chosen shape (it can be an image or a name or anything you want), to have a nice and professional result, all you have to do is to give to each one of it an offset so that it's larger than the next.So, just for a basic cut, you are also going to need some transfer tape, which you can easily find on Amazon.

It is better to have a cheap tape as well, so that you can tape down the layer. Make sure that the result is nice and flat with no wrinkles, and then take your transfer tape and pass over your hand to make sure that is nice and flat as well. Now, you have to burnish down the front of it with your hands, peel that up, burnish down the back too and then you want to peel away the carrier sheet though that the vinyl was on, and leave the vinyl behind on the transfer tape.

Marketing Cricut for Beginners

Now you are going to peel up the second layer making sure that your design is staying down on your transfer tape, and peel and again but slowly making sure each step of the way, leaving your design both layers behind on. Now that you have the two layers together, let's take the layer three. Take this vinyl and tape it down on your pad and then lay down the two unified layers. You must be really careful when you are doing this because you have one shot, once you have touched the surface of the vinyl, you can't go back and try again.Pass your hand over and make sure it is thicker and not just laying down because it is easy to make bubbles in it and then smooth it out any bubbles as you go.Now carefully take off the tape making sure you are not damaging your design. So again burnish it down and take out slowly the carrier sheet, and so do the exactly the same way with fourth layer. The final result is amazing!

How to cut something that is larger than your mat

When you start to get used to the Cricut you can't stop your imagination. So you want to create something special for your parties, for example for Halloween you can create images bigger that will go against your window, there are loads of images that you can find on Google, all you have to do is to turned any images in to vector file.So, from the Cricut Design Space you can change the height to 25 inches.Go to shapes and take the square. My cardstock for example is 8,5 by 11, so you are going to unlock it and a change the size of that square, then you make duplicate of that square, because those multiple squares are what we are going to use to cut the big image that you have chosen, for example a zombie silhouette.Take one of those squares put it on the part of the image that you want to cut, I would recommend the head first. Select and take the piece of the head and put it apart on the right side of the screen for now. Then do the same for each piece of the silhouette. You will obtain pieces like a puzzle and then you just set up your cricut and start cutting. Once you have done the cutting you start to tape them up, and you have your big size zombie silhouette.

How to deal with Wood

Marketing Cricut for Beginners

Let's talk about using Cricut for wood creations. If you are a complete beginner you might wonder how it is possible to make original crafts and how far you can go with it. Well, you can be sure that nowadays you can create nearly anything from home. All you need is a Cricut machine! Wood is cuttable with your Cricut, well some type of wood is more appropriate than others, but remember that you can also iron-on or attach vinyl on your wood, as I always say there is no limit to your creations! When talking about wood, I want you to be more careful than usual, because everybody knows that wood can be expensive but if you pay a little bit of attention around you can find wood cheaper if not free. To help you with this I want you to consider two characteristics that wood must have: the strength of the wood and its durability. So, after you make a fair distinction about it, start to recycle wood every time you get the chance to do it

Marketing Cricut for Beginners

If there is nothing you recover from your house or garage, why not asking to your neighbors? Why not going to flooring companies, or construction companies? Why not trying with Craiglist? Many people have extra stuff and have no space to store it, there you can find great deals!Woodworking can be really rewarding, more than others, it is totally different than working with vinyl, cards, t-shirts, etc... It is another planet, you have to find out if it is what you are looking for.Take the time to watch the various woodworking videos available on YouTube. You can find valuable information and get new ideas for projects you may never have considered before. Cricut Knife Blade is not super fast but that is what you want to use to make beautiful jobs of cutting. You need to calibrate your Cricut Knife Blade as first thing. Make sure you calibrate by following the Cricut step by step guide, but if you are in trouble with it you will find many videos about it, so do not worry. Make sure you use some blue painter's tape or masking tape because you will use this tape to secure your material to your Strong Grip Mat when prepping for a cut, so just tape all four sides of the mat and go ahead

Marketing Cricut for Beginners

You can start easy, by trying to do alphabet letters or simple figures on your mat of your Cricut Design Space.The material I recommend to use is balsa wood, you can find several different colors of it and if you can't find what you are looking for, you can always stain it.You connect to your Cricut machine and search for the wood material that you are going to use. Check and make sure that all the white stars on your rotating bar of the Cricut machine are all pulled to the right hand side, this will prevent from marking up the wood, furthermore if you want to avoid the risk of breaking your blade remember that the smallest pieces of your design, especially the interior of those pieces need to be greater than ¾ of an inch, and any line that you have needs to be larger than the diameter of a pencil because the blade may not cut cleanly in those particular cases. And there you go, you press go and watch your Cricut machine do its work. You can create so many projects, so many ornaments for any event. Tip: There is something that you might not be aware about and that is really interesting, in fact, when you are cutting the wood with your Cricut, you should know that you can add one more pass

Marketing Cricut for Beginners

In fact, when the Cricut Maker completes a mat you can check the cuts of your design. And if it hasn't cut all the way through, you can send it through once more. If the machine stops cutting can be different reasons, for example could be because of minor defects on your material, or your blade has jammed. Check if the "C" button is flashing, if so brush off the debris and press it again. If you could not find the wood of your favorite color, you can also decide to stain your woods, as said, I recommend you to wear gloves for this process; you can gently rub your wood ornaments with a paper towel moistened with gel stain of your preferred color.

The Design Space is an Internet application that helps companies develop business strategies.

For business, you may want to make t-shirts with your Cricut. You can create the shirts with three steps.

Now you have to resize the picture to fit onto your T-shirt. You need both side of the picture in the same size and then press "OK".

After resizing, you need to attach all of the elements. Once you have attached the all, you are ready to begin the cutting and weeding process.

Now your design is ready to be put on a T-shirt. You can use either a regular iron or the Easy Press 2.

Marketing Cricut for Beginners

Before clicking Make it, in order to ensure you that all of the words remain in the order you see it on the canvas area, I recommend you to select all of the layers, and then click on Attach located at the bottom of the Layers panel. Many people adopt this method to create their t-shirts. But I like comfy life, and if you are so too, I recommend you to use T-shirt templates to see how your work will come up when it will be finished. This will give your more the idea if you are doing well, especially in combining colors. Don't get confused, it is to find. To add your favorite template, all you have to do is clicking on the templates button on the left panel of the Canvas area.

When you are happy with your design you are able to proceed to cut. When you start the process of cutting, the template is there for you to help to visualize, so when you start the process of cutting, the template disappears.

Tip: When you use the Heat Transfer Vinyl or Iron on project, make sure that you turn the Mirror option. Then your machine will cut.

For Christmas

For the classroom

For gifts

Free

For cups

For wedding

Signs

Wood

"I know you want to see how far you can go with your imagination. You can make a lot of stuff from your material, and that is why you have so much material! If you can create anything, there is no limit to what you could make."

If you don't have all the tools, look for a solution. You should take one step at a time. It's not just about woodworking, but also about painting and crafting. And then you will get good results.

Develop the trim and put it on the plywood. Make sure that is transported to a workshop with better tools.

Marketing Cricut for Beginners

Create edge boundaries and fight patterns to draw several of the terror from painting, staining, as well as covering.

Remind yourself of the portion ID as well as rotation when producing a tremendous assembly challenge on a CNC, laser beam cutter, or maybe chop saw. (Peel and ignore once the task is actually assembled.)

Get bed sheets and vinyl that are used for water or solvent based paints. You will need them if you want to paint.

Create stencils and resist levels for chemic etching or maybe sandblasting on metal sheets, acrylic, glass, or wood.

Dollar tree

For baby

Card stock

Décor

You can test stiff paper or produce foam prototypes of product designs to ensure a smooth design process. Ambitious CNC and laser cutters slice in miniature, which will help you contain your budget for executing on costly or large materials. Add patches, decals with weathering, and textured color onto 3d printed replica props that are fussy or small too using the printer of yours!

Sometimes the most effective slices are hidden, so you need to use double-stick adhesive sheets. These will securely attach your decorations to your project or even to walls and tables.

For kids

Marketing Cricut for Beginners

Creating new things with your kids can be amazing. You will see how crafting can bring joy to them and for all family members too! Kids love getting stuff they are proud of, which they show their friends or also personal school supplies. But you don't have to craft just animals - feel free to use this technique on many other Cricut crafts like printing out pictures and cutting them into shapes so that the children can easily glue everything together, creating paper cutouts home decoration themselves without help from mommy/daddy...

Creating a new thing with your kid is pretty epic because it brings happiness not only in his life but more importantly in yours as well. Children often get really excited when given something- anything-they're able tto

You can have fun with your kids by creating foods, like ice cream, cakes and pizzas with many different tastes, it is up to them! Want a fun party game that also doubles as a Cricut Craft for kids? Create "Pin the Elephant" game! You want your kids to study more? Challenge them with prizes. Create mouse bookmarks. If you have old fabric to cycle up, get a fun activity out of it. Create a scrap matching game with Cricut Iron-on.

Marketing Cricut for Beginners

Teaching our children to reuse is so important. Help your kids make their own backpacks from old ones or even cardboard boxes! Kids love decorating and will have a blast making something new out of trash they found around the house, while also learning how recycling can help save the environment. Who knew you could do such an amazing thing with just some tape? Your child's backpack won't be complete without one these sun catchers hanging on it for when summer comes along too!

Some things are not extremely safe to make with your kids, but here few examples of what you can create together without any concern: Magnetic bookmarks, stamps, puzzles, lunch-notes, canvases, mini diary notes for kids, etc…Boys love their cars, so why don't you create toy cars, they'll love to project them with you even more since they get to personalize them with their names. Make it a race among the kids who can finish first. So many things you can create for and with your kids, also pop-up books, window cling dartboards, paper airplanes, hopscotch mats, and so on…ouser

No matter what it is your children will always be thrilled as long as they get to personalize it themselves in some way. Design space lets them do just that and gives them hours of fun time designing something new every day!

Farmhouse

The Farmhouse style is a nod to a time when life was simpler—and people lived with less. Keep the designs simple and classic, using neutral palettes for painting walls or choosing clothes that match your décor - even if it's just an accent piece. Whether you're looking to make wood signage or trendy farmhouse shirts, stationary, use this list I compiled below for inspiration:

Farm sweet farm

Grateful

Eat

Simply blessed

Welcome

Family

Thankful

Less is more

Kitchens are for gathering families

Gather

Blessed

Laundry

Home sweet home

Gathering room

Kitchen

Pantry

Loved

Farmer's Market

Bless this farmhouse

Our farmhouse

Home sweet farmhouse

Marketing Cricut for Beginners

Bless this nest

Live simply

Good eats

Relax

Wash

Soak

Be Humble and Kind

Love

Stay awhile

Live more, worry less

Farm Fresh

Dairy

These are the good old days

Be our guest

Farmhouse

Marketing Cricut for Beginners

Meals & Memories Made Here

Unwind

General store

Homestead

Joy comes with the morning

There's no place like home

If you can be anything, be kind

Fresh farm (eggs, meat, chicken, etc)

Enjoy the little things

Homemade

Happiness is homemade

Market fresh produce

Fresh baked goods

Faith, family, and farm life

Life is better on the (porch, swing, farm)

For this family, we are grateful

Fresh brewed coffee

Farmhouse life

Be still and know

Shiplap

Today is a good day for a good day

Do small things with great love

Home is where your herd is

Let's stay home

Paper

Paper-cutting is a very old art form that dates back thousands of years. In our modern world, it has been translated into intricate designs and patterns for cards, invitations, scrapbooks along with other papercraft projects. With just some parchment or maybe standard office papers as well as your scissors in hand you can create all sorts of things like kirigami or origami - the list goes on!

Marketing Cricut for Beginners

Iron-on

Ironing on a Cricut can be tricky. We have found that if you follow these steps, it will make the process much easier:

First thing to do is set your iron to Cotton/Linen setting and then turn OFF steam for any type of steam irons- this means you should not use dry or wet cloths with one either. Preheat the material where weeded images are placed by using an iron at least 10 seconds before applying cut image liner side up onto preheated area.

Then you can put the iron-on sheet, liner side down, onto Cricut Standard Grip cutting mat. Select and Size the images(s) you want to cut.

Generally, you do not mirror adhesive vinyl. But if you're using HTV (heat transfer vinyl), you DO mirror your image before you cut and be sure to place your vinyl glossy side down or dull color side up on the mat.

The reason that you need to mirror your design when working with heat transfer or iron on vinyl,

Marketing Cricut for Beginners

You cut the design on the back side of the vinyl.

HTV has a clear plastic carrier sheet that covers the top of the vinyl, and the other side is where the heat-sensitive adhesive is (it is not sticky or tacky to the touch)

Don't worry, you can use a household iron to apply your heat transfer vinyl. ...

Some HTV does apply at different settings, but standard heat transfer vinyl should be applied on the "linen" setting of your household iron. Regular SiserEasyWeed Heat Transfer Vinyl (HTV) can be cut using the "Iron-On" setting on the dial of a Cricut Explore machine. To customize for thicker material like our Glitter HTV, set it to Custom mode and adjust accordingly when cutting out designs with shapes or detailed lines in them that are not straight edges.

Stickers and Labels

Stick physical numbers or maybe time labels directly onto the dining room table while you photograph the phases of other processes. You can make stickers and sticky notes at your preference- there are loads of things you can create, from a love phrase to a warning.

Cricut for Business

Mindset

I'm so excited to share all of the ways you can make an impact right here in your community! Maybe that's by starting a small business, teaching others what you've learned from years on the job or maybe just giving back. I hear there are plenty of families locally who need help with childcare and elderly care for their loved ones? And don't forget about building some real estate equity while we're at it too!

Marketing Cricut for Beginners

One of the many ways in which you can make money is by working for yourself. It's been shown that people who work at home are happier than those who go to a traditional office every day, and it doesn't take as much time or effort on your part!

Hey, you're all here because you want to make a change in your life or someone else's and I'm going to show the way. So first of all there are three types of people who are out there: The ones that think it will be too hard for them- don't worry about those, they'll never get anywhere anyways; then the hopeless type- just give up on these guys cause if they really wanted this badly enough than perhaps something would have worked by now but hey what do we know? Lastly comes our category which is most likely where any one with even an ounce of grit belongs - so keep reading!

You have to think of yourself as a bamboo tree. Do you know about bamboo trees? I was completely shocked when I discovered that this amazing plant stays in its seed form for five years, yes FIVE YEARS! And all the time is just underneath there not doing much but it's building roots and other stuff--building its foundation for growth.

And then after those five long years if it's taken care of during that whole time and everything goes right...it grows 90 feet in six weeks: exponential growth. But you need to take care of yourself like your own personal garden or else nothing will happen."

So the question is, how long did it take for that tree to grow 90 feet? It took five years in six weeks. Every single bit of that process is what was required for that tree to grow. Okay. And if it didn't, like if you don't take care of that tree for those five years, if you don't take care of you of what you want to do, your plan, your project, your business, well it's not going to grow.

Now, in this part of the book you are going to see the essentials to get started with the whole business, you are going to see what makes a successful product even if you want to go online.

You have to be able to get inside the mind of your potential customer. Remember, especially online, the two things you got is your product and your listing. Online, remember the only thing you got is your listing. They can't touch, feel, taste, your product, none of that. It's all just those photos in those descriptions and, soon or later, reviews. So you got to put all your effort and time into those when you get started.

Cricut Business has exploded through the digital world!

In today's world, if you don't advertise on the Internet, you will miss a lot of business. It doesn't matter if you are good at Cricut or not. You need to be online anyway.

Marketing Cricut for Beginners

Every small business owner needs to sell products or services, and the best way is through advertising. You really are in luck because today you have a plethora of options that can help your company get noticed by more people than ever before! These days you don't just advertise locally; this generation has their eyes peeled for new businesses wherever they may be located. And good news: with social media platforms like Twitter, Facebook and Instagram marketing campaigns are easier than ever. What's even better? A lot of these sites offer different types of ads so if TV commercials aren't working out for your industry then try something else - anything could work nowadays!

When you create a website, like an e-commerce trade, you are letting people buy your products without having to go to your store. But there is more than one way to make this work. You can use a Website builder or hire someone else who knows how to do it.

People who don't know about your business can see your website now. They can research it and ask you questions.

Marketing Cricut for Beginners

The Internet is a good way to grow your business. You can advertise there and do more things.

In recent years, the e-commerce trades as raised a steady twenty-five every year, and experts feel that this trend will continue. When you finally decide to take the plunge and get your business started on the Internet, there are a few steps that you should take before starting. This will be a nerve wrecking, nail biting point in the growth of your business.

What's the point of starting a business without doing any research first? If you're considering jumping in, make sure to do some preliminary work before diving headfirst into e-commerce. Find out what types of businesses are successful online and crunch numbers for your own type. It'll be worth it!

Let me tell you that you are better than other beginners because at least, you know which direction you are taking. You want to work with your Cricut!

It is really much easier to manage a store or anything online related to your interests, it cannot be denied.

Marketing Cricut for Beginners

Creativity and patience can overcome any obstacles.

It is true that it will be more complicated for a creative who does not know how to work with materials such as wood, but creativity combined with time and perseverance are enough to solve even seemingly insurmountable problems.

This is because if you have knowledge of the topic covered in your niche, you will be able to more easily recognize the elements of value to offer to your potential customers. The more specific and specialized you are the more you win over your competitors.

You will be able to identify the best products to market, using qualitative and high-level descriptions. And don't think you are limited because you are using your Cricut and it is not a professional tool, because with it and coordinating with the help of some local professional like a carpenter r a tailor or else you are can be sure you can create many tangible and intangible items that result to be very professional and good looking.

You will be able to answer even the most technical and complex questions your customers will ask you and it will be much easier to identify all the elements to be used to get a better grip on the public.

Brainstorming Section

Everyone loves buying something original, anything completely different as opposed to the others, and all collectors who have bought an item of any kind can tell you how special it feels. Crafted items are starting to be very popular each day because they take time and passion that manufactured products lack. It really works with an internet application called the Design Space. With this machine there is no limit to what you can do - just design or buy a design and then make it your own by resizing for example!

As Benjamin Franklin supposedly once said, "If you fail to plan, you are planning to fail."

So, go with this very useful step by step essential guide to start your business and don't quit until you made it.

Phase 1

Marketing Cricut for Beginners

1. Think and write down your plan of action. There is no path for those who don't have clue where they are going to.

The first things you need to determine are:

-What kind of product you're going to sell,

-What type of customers you're going to reach,

-How you are going to find them.

For example: you want to sell customized woods for little coffee shops or little farms. You don't want to take risk, so it is better to test in your local area to see how it goes.

2. Search about your competitors

What your competitors top-selling products are

How much they charge for their products

What channels (online or offline, or both) your competitors are using for marketing

Find out where your competitors are lacking

Marketing Cricut for Beginners

You need to take your time and make a marketing research about your competitors success and about their products.

Phase 2

Cost of Materials –

You have to try to only buy as much material as you might need but don't get discouraged because it is never perfectly optimized.

1. Make sure the cost of material is actually at a bare minimum,

-consider also all the activities involved, which includes manifacturing, purchasing, and delivery

-the quality of the material and the final product must be high enough to satisfy the customer need

there is going to be some unused scraps and material when buying in bulk.

Phase 3

Marketing Cricut for Beginners

Who do you sell to? What should you sell? Where can you sell it?

I know that you are excited to start selling your products, but it is important to take responsible steps before starting.

Many of your business decisions will depend on your target audience, so it is essential to identify your target audience, first.

For example, if you r Business Idea is to create Menu Boards, your possible Target Audience can be restaurants or coffee shops in your city

Phase 4

Testing your Business

You don't want to create a product that nobody wants to buy, or that would be a complete waste of your time, money and resources.

If you want to succeed in your business you need to take responsible steps and you can test the market to see if people will actually want to buy what you plan to sell. So, give some try by producing few prototypes to offer your unique products to some of potential buyer and see how they react.

Marketing your Cricut

Understanding your customers and where to find them is important in any market. By breaking down the different groups, you can gauge which places are best for marketing – whether it be on Facebook or at a local event.

Understanding how your customer base breaks into two segments will help determine what type of advertising techniques work best for both B2B and B2C environments - from advertisements on social media sites like Twitter or Instagram to attending networking events with businesses that have similar products as yours.

Marketing Cricut for Beginners

If you want to sell with your own website, it's best to choose between one of these two segments and focus on that. If you are going for online sales, this will require a higher technical knowledge base but don't worry if programming isn't in the cards- there's lots we can do without being programmers! For example, providing quality custom work or becoming an information hub (or bulk offering provider). Either way: pick one niche and invest all your time into getting results fast because they'll come soon enough once you have momentum up.

If you decide to provide custom work, don't also try to become an information hub at the same time. After establishing your initial footing, and getting profitable sales,

Business to Business

The cost of a product is directly proportionate to the number produced, so if you want your products at an affordable price point for customers, make sure that productivity and efficiencies are maximized during production.

The opportunities are fewer, and the client expectations are higher. So for this reason I recommend to start an easy path.

Marketing Cricut for Beginners

There are many people who do not know how to balance their finances and those that don't take care of this aspect will find themselves overwhelmed by the number-crunching at some point. One way you can prevent a situation like this is using online accounting software, which should help with your financial management needs. You may also want to invest in other tools for saving money too!

Here are some of good ideas that you are able to create easily once you get familiar with your Cricut and make and sell for additional cash.

Keychains

Rustic Signs

Laptop, mobile phone Cases of different colors

Car and motor stickers

Monogrammed stuffs

Food Trays

Calendars

Pic nic sheets

Monogrammed dishes

Doormats

Menu Boards

Leather Gadgets

Water Bottles

Canvas Wall Art

Personalized Jewelry

Understanding E-Commerce in Your Cricut Business

It is nearly impossible to learn how to E-commerce your Cricut creations in just one day. You will need many books and many days to learn this.

Marketing Cricut for Beginners

In the world of e-commerce, it's always important to remember these 4 keys. These are your fundamentals in order for you be successful at any stage or point that you may encounter. First and foremost is social media marketing which will help promote a brand with an engaged following who can refer potential buyers their way as well as provide valuable insight on what people like about your products/services so they feel more comfortable purchasing from you! Second up is SEO (search engine optimization) which helps drive traffic towards sites via keywords such things key words, meta tags all those good stuffs; thirdly I want to mention content marketing because this one has been my bread and butter recently when promoting blog posts about anything related to retailing fashion items online;

ü Flexibility

ü Ease of use

ü Scalability

ü Security

ü Flexibility

Marketing Cricut for Beginners

Researchers have found that when you offer gifts or items to your customers, they will be more likely to buy from you. You need an e-commerce solution that can change how much the gift is or give a coupon for their next purchase.

Also, if your product comes in a variety of models or styles, with different options and different prices then you must communicate these factors and portray them distinctively in your online store. A true business person will certainly follow the patterns of his or her usual clients as well as those who directly visit the site. Web statistic tracking tools can be a great help to this end.

ü Ease of Use

Some e-commerce stores are very easy to use and require only a few minutes to learn while others are more complex with so many features that they can be overwhelming. Being able to see a demonstration of software before buying it is a great help to determining ease of use.

ü Scalability

Marketing Cricut for Beginners

Choosing the right e-commerce solution can be a daunting decision, but it's important to keep in mind that you'll need one capable of changing with your needs. If you pick something too simple now and then grow out of it later on, not only will conversion rates suffer (due to having more trouble than necessary converting all inventory), but so might search engine rankings as well! That's why picking an option able to change alongside your company is key for success.

For example, some stores owners may not want coupons in the beginning but then down the road decide it is a good idea. Some stores may also have limits on number of products, inventory control and tracking that down the road will be very important.

ü Security

Of utmost importance to online stores is transaction security. The priority for any business firm should be secure transactions. Thanks to Netscape for introducing SSL (secure socket layer), data can be protected by online store owners. SSL is an encryption technology that encrypts a message and the receiver decrypts it by using RSA security. To enable SSL on your web server you need a digital ID (a form of identification that will recognize you). Many web hosts provide SSL installation for anywhere from a few bucks to a few hundred bucks per year.

Overall, you want flexibility, ease of use, security and scalability in your online store. I recommend you to research your options before you make a final choice, and whenever possible, get a free trial of your solution before you buy.

It is possible to create your own design on the Design Space with ease.

The Social media is also crucial in the development of this type of business. If you are able to effectively promote your products, you can achieve important performances.

If you are a beginner, aiming for a continuous publication on Instagram and Facebook is already a good start, but if you want to really sell you must go for Etsy and develop your own business online with your own website.

Whilst to manage with success social media it is very important to be consistent in your publications trying to involve your users with "Call to action", or posts that invite surfers to interact with your page.Example: "Tag a friend you might like ...". By creating your own website, selling on Etsy and pinning on Pinterest will not surely make you busy at same way, unless you are selling very much, of course.

In case you are keen of managing the social media, keep in mind that the Call to Action(s) allow to improve the engagement of your users letting you build a real rotating community in your store, and who knows..., in the future to create a real brand.

For social publishing you can think of relying on the Social Rabbit plug-in which will allow you to automate your social posts allowing you to save a significant amount of time.

Choosing the Right Domain Name

Domain names are to websites as book covers are to novels. They must be both creative and keyword-rich if you want your website in the search engine listings, yet create an alluring first impression for visitors who may not have seen it before. Read on about how a domain name can achieve this delicate balance of creativity and optimization!

Marketing Cricut for Beginners

The first step to choosing a catchy domain name is finding the perfect keyword. A good place to start would be with your website's goal; you can find keywords that are relevant by plugging them into an analyzer and seeing what kind of options come up. If it turns out that all but one of the phrases in question fit well within your site, then go for whichever phrasing best summarizes its purpose!

This is because when it comes to search engine optimization, more specific keywords are better since they are less likely to be used by other webmasters. uo sould find the perfect keyword for your site, then you can search on google to see which keywords and phrases are related to that point.

Keyword research is a fundamental part of any website optimization strategy since it's so important in determining how people will be able to find your website. Google Analytics has built-in tools that are very useful when conducting keyword research; this data can also help you figure out what content should go where or even who might want to advertise with you!

Marketing Cricut for Beginners

Best practices include not only picking words relevant to the type of work your company specializes in but also avoiding unfavorable phrases like "buy" or "cheap."

Now you can start selecting a domain name for your website. Most providers will allow you to see whether or not that domain is available. If it isn't, they'll tell you what domains are similar and if one of those ends in .com, go with it! Otherwise be more creative when picking out the perfect URL for your site because getting stuck on this step could mean trouble down the road.

For example, you can use 'filler' words, numbers or phrases within your domain name to still include your selected keyword. Fillers could be 'a,' 'an' or 'the.' Search engines tend to not look at these words, so you still have a good shot at getting indexed while having a domain name that is memorable and catchy. You can also consider fillers at the end of a phrase, such as '101'.

When you're trying to break into the Internet, it's best not to think of yourself as small potatoes. That's why a lesser-used extension could work wonders for your site and company - because those keywords are often so popular they can't be ignored. .net, .biz or org may seem like too much commitment right now; but hey! They might just get you that all important ranking boost in Google USA when nobody else will do the trick.

In conclusion, choosing a domain name that will get the right buzz from both humans and search engines doesn't have to be hard. The keyword analyzer will help you with 90% of your domain name, while your wit with fillers can help you the other 10%. And, if after an immense amount of pondering, you still can't get the .com, you can opt for other extensions.

When choosing what crafts to sell, there are a few points to consider

Marketing Cricut for Beginners

When you first start your online business, the most important question is what are you going to sell? There are several things that can be created and sold with a Cricut machine. You will find many videos about it on YouTube, as well as ideas of projects in Google search results when googling "Cricut." However if this seems like too much work there's always something easier: selling others' creations! If you're not graphic designer or don't know how to create files for use with the Cricut software but have an eye for design then why not make some money just by creating graphics other people could buy?

People are always looking for people who make good Cricut designs, not everybody is design savvy and a lot of people just want to be able to make beyond this initial phase of designing.

So there are many questions you have to ask yourself to set your business with Cricut.

Points to consider when deciding the answer to that question are:

· Is it a tangible item I want to sell?

· Is it light and easy to ship?

Marketing Cricut for Beginners

· Is it a digital good that is downloaded?

· Is it perishable or fragile?

· Is there enough demand to make your venture profitable?

· Does it have little competition from large online companies (niche products)?

The last characteristic is the one that can be hard to pin down or else it can be your point of advantage, because crafts products win it all in my opinion, always.

Here is a generally accepted method of arriving at an idea of how heavy the demand and competition is for a product.

If you have a special interest in some products that meet the above criteria, great, but don't limit your investigation just to items you like. You are looking for a niche product with relatively good demand (enough to make it profitable), but without heavy competition.

One way to see what the demand is for products you are interested in is to look at search engines to see how frequently people search for the product you are considering.

Marketing Cricut for Beginners

Research has shown that it is more beneficial to focus on a niche and offer products in one category with the widest variety possible. This will allow you not only to rank higher, but also become the best online shop for this product type since there is little supply compared to demand. For example instead of selling general craft supplies, sell needlepoint kits which are much less available than other options such as balloons or magnets.

The result from all research should be that one or more products would fit into a small niche market - many people want these goods because they have limited availability so your store can capitalize off their uniqueness by offering them at an affordable price point while still maintaining high quality customer service standards.

Quality, technical characteristics, specifications, prices, all factors to consider when choosing the products to import into your e-commerce.

Carefully analyze all these factors using one of the most powerful tools to carry out this type of evaluation or customer feedback.

The reviews can actually provide you with even more precise indications of the descriptions offered by the suppliers regarding the quality of the products.

It might also be useful to buy yourself a couple of products to actually understand if the items offered by a particular supplier are actually qualitative.

Once identified, you can proceed with their import in your store.

<u>Pay attention to the size.</u> If it is a tangible item, what you want is selling a creation that is handy and easy to ship. Nothing too big or dangerous. You need to avoid everything to delay the time of the shipment or to compromise it. The general rule is that a good product should be able to fit inside a shoebox and weigh less than 2kg (4.4lb), the weight limit for ###a href="https://www.salehoo.com/blog/what-is-epacket-shipping" rel="noopener noreferrer" target="_blank">ePacket. This is to save you paying extra for shipping. Stick with it!

Marketing Cricut for Beginners

<u>It is better to create items that are in demand all year round</u>. This is an ideal of the product you will decide but still it is not a must. In fact, selecting a product that you would sell typically for one season a year it is not a big deal because you won't sell during the rest of the year.

If you want to sell welll would recommend to choose products of a price range between 13$ and 220$. If the price is too low you're not going to be making much of a profit margin. And going over 220$ a so high price will discourage people buying.

So, once you have decided about your niche, and please try to choose a niche that is not already done and overplayed, I would try to come up with something different and sell it on Etsy and pin the Pinterest. You can also sell things on eBay, Facebook groups, but in this case I recommend going on your local area groups or in handmade themed groups. Last but not least, take good picture!

If you think that the affiliation is the most suitable option for you, that one is a good idea too. If you are an online passionate, or you are a blogger, or you have an online presence and want to share deals, make your own tutorials for them or you have a quite big following on the internet you can become an affiliate. You can create an affiliate link and if anyone wants to buy the Cricut they can buy it through your link and you will make a little bit of money. This affiliation program is accessible from anyone though.

Selecting supplies for business

The role played by supplies is absolutely crucial to success. The more precious are the materials you use for your Cricut creations the more value your items will acquire and you can point to sell at higher price for good quality.

From it depends your customer satisfaction.

The key Points in setting your products:

- what makes the product unique

- the value the product brings

- story behind the product (story why you are selling this product)

The main thing with selling your own products is that all of the responsibility is on your shoulders. You can only sell as much as you make, so you have to invest your own time into production.

The main benefit is that, aside from the cost of materials and your time, you don't have to make a significant investment up front. You also don't have to rely on suppliers. It's all on you.

How to Choose the perfect Name for your Cricut Business

Marketing Cricut for Beginners

Choosing a Business name can be vital to the success especially for a website since you are at the beginning I will pay particular attention to this chapter.

So before you start the first thing I recommend you to do is to do some research on the Internet.

Try to find a name that is original, standing out from the others, you will have that name for years so it is better that you are really convinced. Make sure your name can grow with your business, a name that makes sense to you but should make sense to the public as well, so envision your name before finalizing it. Name should be easy to remember, memorable and spellable.

Next you will need a logo for your business that includes one of the most common elements in marketing such as words, colors, shapes or pictures.

Marketing Cricut for Beginners

You can use an online software which is simple and has some good features built-in but it also allows you to build custom logos with more control over style options than other websites I have seen. You could also hire someone on Fiverr who would create an original high quality design for $20-$30 USD per hour if you are short on time or funds or both!

Once you know what your company's name and logo looks like then start building up your website content by writing about yourself.

Your Business name, will be also the same as for the domain of your website.

A solid keyword domain name is the key to establish a strong presence and making the resources of the Internet more reachable. With a great name, it's always easy to reach new and existing clients.

The keyword domain name is the main thing if you want to establish a strong presence and making the resources of the Internet more reachable.

Marketing Cricut for Beginners

Having a great name, can make it always easy to reach new and existing clients. Therefore, a number of companies are ready to spend a large amount of money to get hold of and promote a good keyword rich domain name.

In order to take advantage of search engine traffic, people choose keyword domain. By selecting a domain that is equivalent to a keyword search, websites are able to rank higher for targeted keywords and thus benefit from added traffic and more potential clients. Whether to opt for a brandable domain or a keyword domain is a choice one must make in accordance with their business plan.

Follow these simple rules to maximize the benefit of a keyword domain, accomplish success in directory submissions, and enhance site keyword density:

Structuring

Order the URL (Uniform Resource Locator) in such a manner that more vital keywords are listed before those that are less important. For example, if he target keyword is "money" then money-online.com would be more effectual than online-money.com.

Marketing Cricut for Beginners

Length

1. A majority of studies confirms that a number of people use two words or more in a search; as a result phrases are very useful.

2. Always stick to two-three keywords, with hyphens in between.

3. A lengthy, complex URL is more likely to be rejected by directory editors' sites from which one would like to receive links.

Correct English and Must Make Sense

1. In order to execute directory submissions and link popularity campaigns, the URL should be grammatically correct.

2. When examined by an editor, "money-online-white.com" might sound like a less-reliable resource while "white-money-online.com" sounds more justifiable and is less likely to be questioned.

Put together "power words"

Marketing Cricut for Beginners

In order to create a distinctive domain name that is still available, one way is to add another less important word to the mix. A few examples include: now, top, just, go to, pro, guide, online and find etc.

Avoid using most popular keyword phrases

There is intense competition for keywords in the marketplace, so stay away from the most popular keyword phrases. It is impractical to think that a new website could rank number one on a popular phrase like "Shop Online". A number of well-known companies who have been on the Internet for a few years will have the big advantage of link popularity and click popularity.

Try to register a .com domain

Always use ".com". In case it is a business website, avoid using domains ending with "ru" or "org". At once, one can consider registering a ".net" domain, but as most people are familiar with ".com", it is better to stick to convention.

In addition to the above, an understanding of the domain name system (DNS) is also vital while choosing a domain name. The DNS is set up to make regular words map to IP (Internet Protocol) addresses. In order to connect all computers on the Internet, an IP address is used by networks. A domain name can be up to sixty-three characters, comprising of letters, numbers, or the dash symbol. For example, in the world of computer networking, the web address fishing.com becomes the IP address 124.133.1.1. However, it's the domain name that people around the world use when looking for Web sites or sending an e-mail.

Finally, it is very important to choose a keyword phrase very carefully. This can be considered as one of the most critical decisions one will make regarding the success or failure of a website. One must identify the exact phrase that searchers will use to find a website. The more targeted the campaign is, the more increase in sales will be achieved.

Tip:

If you get stuck, on naming your business, don't worry. When you're first getting started you can do a DBA (doing business as) and you can change your business name anytime.

1. What is important is that you check the availability of your company name in your state with ###a href="https://brock.tv/LZM-I-5329" rel="noopener noreferrer" target="_blank">Legal Zoom.
2. Make sure your company name does not infringe on trademark

Avoiding Trademark Infringement When Choosing a Domain Name

Many webmasters erroneously believe that just because their domain name registrar says a particular domain name is 'available' that it truly is. This is not necessarily so. Even if a domain name is physically available, it may not legally be open for use. Why? It's because there might already be a company that has the rights to the keywords used within the domain name.

If this happens yet the webmaster claims the domain name anyway, they are at risk of losing it through a domain name arbitration proceeding. They could even be charged with trademark/copyright infringement if things get really ugly. For this reason it's best to make sure the keywords used in a domain name aren't protected for someone else. This article will explain how webmasters can make such a determination.

First, webmasters need to check and see if their chosen domain name resembles any existing trademark that is on the books. They will want to do this before actually investing any money in the domain name. To search existing trademarks, webmasters can visit the website of the U.S. Patent and Trademark Office which is USPTO.gov. From here they can search a database that contains current trademarks as well as those that are pending.

If a domain name is similar to a registered or pending trademark, webmasters need to evaluate whether the domain name is still worth taking. Usually, if a site is not selling the same types of merchandise or services that the other business is selling and the trademark is not popular, a webmaster probably won't get into legal trouble if they decide to go on and register the domain name. To be completely sure, webmasters can run the domain name by a trademark attorney. It shouldn't cost too much for an hour consultation.

Of course, if a webmaster would prefer zero percent risk, they can simply try to think of another domain name. When they go about doing this, they need to be more generic and less creative in what they come up with. Using search engine keywords for a domain name is one such strategy. Webmasters can also look into using dictionary terms. If all else fails they can take a generic term and combine it with a term that is less likely to be taken, such as their first and last name.

Either way, once a suitable domain name has been chosen, webmasters should consider getting it trademarked themselves, especially if they are using it to help brand their business. With an official trademark, a webmaster has more legal power should another company try to take them to court. And since there's no shortage of domain name bullies, (companies that try to steal profitable domain names from smaller enterprises), a webmaster should use all legal avenues available to protect the rights of their business.

In conclusion, by checking whether or not a domain name has keywords that are part of a trademark, webmasters lessen the risk that they will have legal problems in the future. If there are problems, and a domain name arbitration proceeding does not rule in a webmaster's favor, they can turn to The Domain Name Rights Coalition.

E- commerce Store – Build your own

Marketing Cricut for Beginners

If you have a product oriented business, the Internet offers a unique ability to reach a broad audience. With new technology, it is easy to build your own e-commerce store.

E-commerce Store

Today's world is an E-commerce (electronic commerce or e-com) world. E-commerce, clearly termed as web commerce, basically means selling of merchandise or services over the Internet with electronic transactions and also through a secure network. E-com is not merely buying and selling or providing services but it is also a method of advertising and marketing through an electronic system as well. E-com also means facilitating the progress of commercial transactions electronically. Right now e-com is a well-established technology in all major countries. In most cases Internet marketing requires you to have your own E-commerce store for maximum return.

<u>Requirements of an E-commerce Store</u>

Marketing Cricut for Beginners

Building an e-commerce store is not an easy job. Software is required that can manage customers as well as their needs. E-commerce software should be able to handle inventory, shipping and handling costs, taxes, dispatching and payment processing of client's orders. You may encounter many options when setting out to build an e commerce store. Before choosing any of them it is important to have a clear view of your requirements. Technical requirements might include coupons, tracking systems, customer login options or any number of other things. Other requirements include what type of impression you want to provide to your valuable clients.

Study the Sales and Marketing Cycle to Determine Your Needs

Marketing Cricut for Beginners

Before you opt for any of solutions for building e commerce store, study the basic model of e commerce that represents the entire sales and marketing cycle. The first building block of this cycle is audience in which you define what type of customers you will target. Second are commodities, in which you characterize the types of products you will put on the market. Third is customer support where you will answer the questions and offer solutions to clients' or potential clients' problems. Next are advertising, marketing and endorsement where a business promotes the products or services. Then there is transaction processing, the most important technical phase of the cycle, which will handle orders, taxes, payment processing and order delivery.

Transactions may be automatic or manual. In manual processing you have to enter credit card information manually through an offline terminal. In the case of automatic processing a client's order form will be setup with a program that processes and charges the credit card for you. After that there are post-deal services regarding how you provide solutions and services after the sale. Last but not least is brand name with which you will create a distinctive business image to correspond with customers. Nobody is going to pay attention to your online store unless something catches their eye.

Refund Policy

We need to talk about the refund policy, privacy policy, terms of service and what you will do. It's up to you what your refund policy is and I for example go the 28 days.

You can make all the points clear, by going to Settings and then check-out, and then scroll down to 'Refund, Privacy, TOS statements'. On the right side you will find the tab 'Generate Sample Refund Policy', click on it and it will generate a Policy automatically that you can customized at your preference.

Or, by using one of online policy generators like www.termly.io, which helps you to create the document step by step. Bear in mind this is all initial stuff, perfect for starting, and that you will need to speak with a consultant or accountant.

Once you are happy with that, just copy it and paste it in your dedicate page.

Let's have a look here the conditions, you should include:

The period of time you send the money back,

What countries are eligible for refunds and returns,

The period of time when customers are eligible for a return,

Items that cannot be returned,

Variants of what they may get: refund only, return and refund, store credit only, exchange only — or some of them, or all of them,

Who pays for shipping, your store or a client,

Your contacts for returns and address the package should be sanded back.

Online Store: the unmissable pages

Then you go filling all the other pages. Add essential pages of your store:

- About us

- FAQs

- Contact us

- Order Tracking

- Shipping and Delivery

- Return Policy

- Privacy Policy

- Terms of Service

Go to Settings and then check-out, and then scroll down to 'Refund, Privacy, TOS statements'. On the right side you will find the tab 'Generate Sample Refund Policy', click on it and it will generate a Policy automatically that you can customized at your preference.

Tips: Loads of people do apply different shipping model. Obviously you can apply whatever you like, but if I can give you a little tip that brought some little more of the flavor of success, Instead of setting the free plus shipping model that a lot of people follow. I would rather offer a standard free shipping on all of my orders. It is easier, avoid confusion and so less headaches.

All you do is put type in, don't type in standard shipping, type of free shipping. Customers will see this at checkout and wherever you can write free shipping. It is a huge factor in your conversion rates and making people buy on your store. If you don't have free shipping, less people are going to make purchases on your store.

How to make your business bigger.

You will be successful with Cricut if you are patient and use the right strategies.

If you stop working especially at the beginning when the results tend to be slow to arrive then you will definitely NOT be able to achieve success with Cricut.

The beginning is the most difficult part as in any type of activity, you will have to be patient and work without seeing any kind of result, committing yourself with the sole aim of being able to see them grow one step at a time.

When you finally see the results coming, you absolutely won't have to stop, but focus on those processes that will allow you to increase them further.

Improving customer experience

It is possible to greatly improve the browsing and purchasing experience of your customers in your store.

The ease of browsing your site will entice your users to come back.

Make sure you make the site fast (Siteground in this for our experience has proved to be the best for now), make payments easy to make, and don't forget to always enter payment terms, shipping terms, return conditions.

It is very important to be extremely honest about shipping times, they must be absolutely aware of the time needed to receive the product purchased.

It is not a big problem for people to wait as long as they are aware that it will still be necessary to do so.

Product catalog update

Always remember to keep offered.

It always analyzes the sales data of the articles, to understand if the products marketed are actually of customer satisfaction or if maybe it may be necessary to study a reorganization of their catalog.

Opening new stores

Marketing Cricut for Beginners

The launch of the first store always represents an opportunity to study the market and acquire those skills that will allow you to really make the strategies to achieve success with Cricut.

Once you have digested this knowledge, why not consider the idea of launching new stores?

You will realize with the successive launches of the enormous quantity of skills acquired with the first store, knowledge that will allow you to achieve the desired results much more easily and quickly.

Explore

There is so much to learn, I can always guarantee it.

For this reason, once you have acquired your personal experience, you will be able to build new strategies based on your specific business history and maybe you can share new winning strategies with the community to achieve success with Cricut.

Being Digital Entrepreneurs also means this, so much and so much research, testing, development and analysis of results.

Marketing Cricut for Beginners

We have finished our journey based on operational steps to achieve success with Cricut.

We hope this guide of ours can help you on your journey, failures on failures have resulted us, but today we can share all that we have learned from our failures hoping that you will appreciate our efforts.

CPSIA information can be obtained
at www.ICGtesting.com
Printed in the USA
BVHW071459210721
612520BV00016B/889